AF441275

the morning

mourner

tales of an average adolescence

zachary hodges

for autumn

may you rest among the stars

<u>prelude</u>

dear reader,

this work is my therapy. thirty poems that revolve around a broken boy as he loves and loses and gushes and grieves; an ode to regret and wrongs and rejection. ultimately, this is a story of making do with what you have. when reading, know that i write to immortalize this moment- a small corner in the building that is my lifespan. consume this work as you wish- flip to any page and read a poem, if you will. but note that there's a story waiting for you between the lines when you're ready for it. the order of the poems is important. take that as a guideline, not a necessity.

i started really writing poetry in the spring semester of my freshman year of college. i took a creative writing course, and it sparked my love of writing- while i've always loved writing, i've never used it as a vessel like i do now. like i said, this is my therapy (although i do also recommend actual therapy). i grieve, i write. i love, i write. i long, i write. poetry is my artistic expression- it's how i've learned to heal amidst all the grievances and joys. and for that, i am thankful.

if you notice, when reading, you may find that part two of the book is very distinct in it's style and dedication. i wrote 'autumn skies' during a time when i was just grieving the loss of a close friend, whom this book is dedicated to. thus, the poetry in that section stands alone amidst the work. while part two works with the rest of the novel and is very important in the overall flow of the story, it also works as a stand-alone piece, and that's something i quite enjoy about the work. take this information as you will.

when reading, please know one thing. i am the morning mourner. i dream of her, sitting on that porch. i watch as he cries confetti tears, and i find a home in his arms (my armoire). i am the broken boy, fearful of becoming a muttering man, grieving the erosion of a rock and settling into a steady avalanche. i sit under autumn skies. i miss her. these are my stories from a corner of my average adolescence.

these are the letters i should've written. i hope they reach their recipients.

here's to more letters.

signed,

the morning mourner

<u>table of contents</u>

introduction:

- dedication
- prelude
- table of contents

part 1: an auburn ploom

- the morning mourner
- a gloveless marriage
- i dream of you
- cotton tree
- it smells of independence
- sensory
- letters i should write
- tightrope
- we look
- abili lane
- headache
- where are you kathy
- star show
- midnight conversation

part 2: autumn skies

- avalanche
- bring me back to december
- midnight drabble
- silence
- only the good

part 3: florida boy

- penance on a porch
- if it were me
- lion head fountain
- immersion
- translucent skin
- sheeran
- empty corner
- am i?
- god, let me bleed
- technicolor astronaut man
- i still get her letters
- florida boy
- dayton, ohio
- gold
- angelina
- apology
- two am walc
- among the stars

part one:

an auburn ploom

<u>the morning mourner</u>

he sits, lukewarm mocha in his hand,   its warmth

reminiscent of   a lover   left behind.

the bells on the door chime as more coffee goers enter—

jing-a-ling,   it sounds,   in a chorus of

quaintness.

the miniscule herd of morning mourners mirror his mind.

low chatter, like an ambience,

and that rich smell, that

pungent smell,   crisp coffee, fresh yet sharp,

crackling through his veins like a drug taking off.

he feels his body restart,   the atmosphere inviting

tension.

the warmth,   the smells.   the chatter.

time inverses, and we fall back into his dorm

room;

the cupboard-sized closet he used to romanticize,

intertwined with

old artworks   and dark blue sheets—

once a place of safety for his average

adolescence.

you.

crying on his bed, come to collect

what you never earned.

what you never

deserved.   tears pool on the dark blue hues.

over and over,

you begging for something that

shouldn't be owed.

his feet firm on the ground, quivering yet

unwavering.

thank god someone reminded him of his worth

before you attempted to rob it.

jing-a-ling, and suddenly, he's back with the

coffee goers.

the morning mourners, the warmth in his hands,

    the pungent smell of coffee replacing yours.

the drug in his body rejuvenates his veins—

    energy surges as his eyes flutter more   and more

awake.

  his body is up, ready to start the day.

    i mourn.

<u>a gloveless marriage</u>

evergreen gloves, two paths conjoined.

  a pair built out of useful design.

watch as they sit, waiting to be worn,

  their love sensible.

a polyester tale of arranged marriage—

  quaint love, born from necessity.

what happens

  to a glove when

    the other is lost?

  the lonely glove,   daft in design

missing an essential element   to its purpose.

  watch as it sits,   unused,   at the bottom

    of a barrel   which contains only hats.

dust collects,   and yet still, i ponder

    where best to use a lonely glove

when it's purpose   has been ripped

    from it's being.

a new day, and   the lonely glove looks up

a hand digs to   the bottom of the barrel,   and rises

       its body from   the crater of carcasses.

    the hand slides in.   (fits like a glove, he muses)

the lonely glove   looks up with dismay, and sees

    a boy,   dawned in cap and coat,   drink in hand.

    the icy drink fills the glove,

        and one hand in pocket, the glove walks out the door,

purpose restored.

i dream of you

     basking in   the glow of fluorescent lighting,

perched atop a chair

     made of charcoal plastic,

your auburn ploom the north star

   amidst   the gray night sky   of ceiling and walls.

i dream of you dancing   to the music

  by the musician

   we both loved,

swaying and vibing to the gospel chords

as if we were there

  when they were written.

i dream of you   in that gown,

the one from   our prom,

so blue that   the hydrangeas wept,

and i too,

for my lungs cried for air,

a heavy reminder to breathe

i dream of you   and   that flannel blanket

the one that now   broods at me

from across the room,

in that letterman jacket that mimics your ploom.

how i wish i could see

it's alliteration in person.

i dream of that auburn ploom showing up at my door

the letterman jacket   dawned to match,

a gospel choir singing   around us,

you taking   my breath away   one last time.

i dream of you and i leaving the lives we made alone, together

i am drunk on dreams.

oh, to make them a reality.

<u>cotton tree</u>

awaken.

see the ceiling, the glass, the hazy white

beyond it—

a tree of cotton,   dusted by the storm,

she lays,

and i with her, a moment of solitude

before   the fog fades   and the storm reemerges.

the storm, the snow…   it floods my brain

said fog fizzles out as i am drowned in memories.

my phone, our group curing ailments   with ales—

hooch filling my system   faster than a flash.

and, a reprise to the flash,

my screen betrays me—

dialing, kindling fires with flames long burnt out.

the heat burns my cheeks as i reach for my

phone, and find one message,

                                        two message, awaiting—

                                                            dear god.

        the cotton melts off the branch;

    my hangover of heartlessness rages on.

                memories emerge in my amygdala,

        and i beg my mind   to forget the words i

once   withdrew—

            the fluttering frozen fractals   just beyond the glass

    mock my hysterics as i yearn to disavow

        the merit   of my memory.

        jesus christ.

        betrayed by my drunken body, i now

understand

    why the snow melts after a relentless storm

                and seeps into the ground,

                            buried in   shame.

. . .

the broken boy and the foggy abyss.

i melt off the tree   like the wispy cotton

and bury myself in the blankets and the dirt,

(without her).

<u>it smells of independence</u>

it smells of

     independence;

hear the birds

  tweeting in the air

      as they fly

   back into

the hemisphere.

feel the grass scratch

         your bare legs,

 bugs biting

    the pale expanse.

it smells of

    faint dewdrops;

  brought on by

a passing storm.

watch them

blend into the fabric

of your black loose shorts;

the youthful blend of

black and blue.

it smells of

summer break;

the last bell

hailing our escape

from boredom

for most,

but for me,   i am bittersweet,

as school was

but a safety

from the tension

outside it.

it smells of

     marching band;

  practice in the summer,

    with

     the chorus of brass and reeds;

snow-tinted

     gatorade energizes

my taste buds

    as i breathe   the springtime air.

it smells of independence.

how i miss

    the days

      when that smell

        brought joy.

loud strokes of volume.

  alarm audio pains my ears

the other kids don't mind it, but i did.

    i cover my ears, they mock me.

      i unplug them.

  the brush of my teeth

    stings my body;

  bristles rub against them.

    i shiver, i shake.

  it doesn't stop. i don't stop.

the cafeteria, roars

  the marching band, soars

  my body jolts from too much touch

  over sensitive, they call me;

i feel too much.

flash forward to adulthood—

the bustling brash of a part-time job

deep breaths and sets of eyes,

i tell myself i'm fine because i'm

'making it up'

there's not a word for how i feel

why would there be?

just a loser in therapy who can't handle

loud crowds and drowned sounds

too much too much   too MUCH.

oh, the life of the undiagnosed.

<u>letters i should write</u>

to tell the world how i feel—

write each individual a letter, a sonnet

a treasure trove of memories

that we shared and will share.

notes are for the weak; power is pounded

in passion—

oh, to write them the world.

some words carry power.

each swish and stroke (and type and text)

deliver pain and passion beyond i could express.

my acidity settles when settled on my keys.

i shuffle throughout language

(the dour coward's sheath).

the grass will never know how their spring

glow refreshes me; the wind

will never feel my gracious repent.

the daffodils will never comprehend

my yearn for their yellow-toned locks.

she will never know how i feel.

. . .

i better get to writing.

<u>tightrope</u>

to see a person

between two towers.

a femme fettered friend

that i knew then. (and now)—

walking on   a clothes wire,

fighting for their life.

i reach out for them,

but i am down under,

several flights and floors

burdened by my mistakes.

lilibeth jude.

their name murmurs in me—

tastes of fresh grapes

from your local basement market.

alone they walk,

and balance,

holding the pressures of

their persistence—

breathing deep, on a tightrope,

with the burdens

thrust upon them.

will they toe the line?

to grow from a seed,

to depart from whence you started,

this is what they know—

to find and fill and love and leave.

they sprout

from their succulent pot,

on a path to smash their potted pen,

to paint their petals

red.

lilibeth jude.

the pesticide kills their weeds.

<u>we look</u>

boredom strikes in my eleventh hour.

sat in a classroom as

the fringe graduate student

lectures on. i cannot focus

(how i love neurodivergence).

my eyes shuffle around the room

as i judge my fellow inmates

as if i were narcissus himself.

i went to high school with you.

well, someone like you

   beanie dawned, hooded in flannel.

masked girls, drowning in cardigan.

  the caricatures in these classes

 mimic the people i once pleased.

   you stare, we look.

i've known you forever.

   we've only met just now.

the passive bell rings,

   and we shuffle out the door.

 i will remember you forever

   in the refuge of my brain.

goodbye, beanie boy.

   hello, eternal curiosity.

<u>abili lane</u>

the boy who lives

    on abili lane

fears the future he might face.

    he's never known a life

beyond sheltered homes and

    rich grasses.

sometimes he looks

    in the mirror

        in the bath

and sees a man in his place.

    how did he get here?

    what led him

        to live in that fluorescent

    dip-dyed hallway?

who dictated

the residents of

abili lane, the

asylum-bent men?

down the hallway street,

he soars,

collecting rabbits

and roaches

he'll carry

for decades.

he hordes

hordes of undead

in his head.

<u>headache</u>

i stand in a bathroom

with shoes too huge

where did i get these?

i shuffle

back to the room we found

back then, and find

friends, from afar

that can only be found

from the follicles of my mind.

oh, to remember a memory

when you're so far removed from it.

will i remember you tomorrow?

i hope so.

we sit under fluorescent lights.

they glare at my hair.

why must the distance

divorce us?

<u>where are you, kathy?</u>

where are you, kathy?

　i don't remember hearing you leave.

　it's scaring me, kathy.

　　your pearls and purses have vanished in thin air,

　as if, by some grace of god, they never existed.

　　where are you, kathy? why are there

　　　pills on the floor, kathy? (or is it chalk?)

　　i'm stumbling around this dim-witted kitchen,

　looking for a sign of who you became.

　　where are you, kathy?

there are no notes on the table,

　　no last messes left behind

　i can't find you, kathy.

　i was promised you wouldn't leave me.

where are you, kathy?

this house feels so cavernous without you.

who did you become, kathy?

the doors of my mind are replaced with prison bars.

what did you do to me, kathy?

i don't even know who i am anymore.

the pills are on the floor, kathy, and

i'm afraid that if i take them,

you won't come back to me, kathy.

i don't know what to do without you.

<u>star show</u>

a vacation for seven,

in the woodlands of my hippocampus,

i watch the stars signal the night.

my thoughts find no comfort

in sleep;

the moon echoes my defeat,

stars serenading.

these wooded log cabin walls

make up a personal planetarium.

i sit in a leather lounge chair

and watch the planets twirl around me—

the star show salsas across the sky,

my eyes following their movements.

the worries of yesterday seem so frail,

so frought,

for tonight, the sky is mine

to dance with around the universe.

my salsa partner holds me

in an everlocking grip.

i rest among the stars.

<u>midnight conversation</u>

"hey… do you hear that sound?"

. . .

"it's gravelly, kind of… gritty."

"i think it's coming from my heater"

. . .

"it's coming from your fridge. or, your heater."

"yeah, no shit."

"i just said that."

. . .

"do you think i should ask someone about it?"

"nah. it doesn't sound life-threatening."

"oh."

. . .

"what if it kills us? what if it, blows up?"

"i wouldn't mind that."

. . .

"maybe, in a week."

. . .

"just... not tonight."

. . .

"yeah, not tonight."

part two:

autumn skies

<u>avalanche</u>

what do you say

     to texts flooding in--

  apologies, and, what happened, and

     who knows, who cares—

because you can't bring yourself to say it

what do you say

     to your coworkers, when you see

  the apologies flashing across your phone,

  and you scroll, and you scroll,   and they

    just   keep   coming.

  she's dead.

  when was the last time you saw her—

     does it matter?

  yes, it does.

oh god, i remember. thank god   we got a photo.

what does it matter that we got

       a photo— who the hell cares?

she's still   not here,   right?

  i should call someone

      but   who?

no one knew her like i did

      well, maybe

   maybe not, but now i'll

  never know

     now i'll never

no.

my rock is gone

       she has e r o d e d .

i am an avalanche

      tumbling down the hill

like she did

      like we did

            like he did once before.

i know this tango.

      i've danced with death

      more times than i can count.

but for the first time,

      i dance alone—

the familiar click of

my light switch

brings me back to

when you were   still with me.

marching bands   and

brassy melodies,

we thought   we ruled the world

and   i'd venture we did.

flashback to   the broken boy,

his foggy abyss

breached by your hold

he screams into   the void

and wonders

what might have been

if you had not been

there to hear him.

"we're too young to be doing this,"

to be playing this game of

funerals and fascists.

watch as we bury you   in a burgundy seal,

the pink   faded from your hair   as i

beg god to   bring it back

bring me back

bring her back.

bring me back to december.

where at least i had a chance.

<u>midnight drabble</u>

these past few nights

      have been sleepless.

home from college,

      in my bedroom,

            surrounded by the things that

            remind me of my youth (and, thus…)

    collecting words   to be heard. down the line;

counting the minutes. until the morning arrives;

thinking of you.

                      midnight rolls by,

    and then one am,

         and then two,

and, suddenly, i'm crying.

i hold the plushie

    you gave me, because

        you aren't

           here

              to

              hold

                me.

  i squeeze.

<u>silence</u>

it's quiet in the suburbs;

a juxtaposition to

college life.

no hum of generators, no faint screams

(they aren't so faint here.)

no horrendous smells or   horrendous actions

only horrendous thoughts .

the silence deafens me as

her echo   speaks;

so jarring that her death

should be deaf.

memories flash,   a youthful array of

the mementos we made.

how to memorialize   your memory,

                    i ponder my choices.

i drown in   memories,

                    my air bubbles art

   in   the name of your

            fleeting face.

oh, to write you   a marching band show,

      with woodwinds and

              wind chimes and

                        motifs from your youth.

      symphonies to   conduct,

                  monuments   to construct;

      poems i'll write,   stories itching to be

                              drafted.

in every direction   i sprawl,

      scrounging and   scratching the floor

for a vice   to fill

the void.

oh, to memorialize you

more than i can mourn.

i vow   to make you

more than a monolith.

"powerful words",   our teacher said

the words   came from me,   sure, but

the power came from you.

phrases flow through me—

i should write them down.

all in due time.

for now,

the silence roars.

i should grieve.

<u>only the good</u>

breathe in,   and smell

the faint sterile scent

of percussive penance;   an echo

of the youthful goodness

that once revolved in

this chamber of solitude.

drag your hands across the grayed floors

it's dirtied status   somehow sentimental

to you,   dressed in gray,

too bright   for a funeral.

trace   the lines   on the walls

and remember   the girl

who once   sat afar.

listen to her echoes,   feel   her tired stance

beg to go back and   change   the   past

to tell her what you found, (much   long   last),   that

you were a sister.

(to the boy dressed in gray)

     you listened to his sorrows,

          when he was so afraid.

     a common struggle connected two strangers

     in this chamber for children—

          and, because of the share,

               he found reason to rise again.

          so help me god, i will make her a martyr

     my marker to mark her into his story;

                    history.

he prays and begs to good gods and bad,

               good god, to strengthen her

                         echo—

his prayers left unanswered.

there is no god.

only the good die young.

part three:

florida boy

<u>penance on a porch</u>

your hair, my face,

  your sweatshirt against my chest,

  getting to know one another.

our friends jeer from inside,

  their excitement around us,

   but we sit in silence.

  warm wooden floors,

our feet graze on top

  nudging each other sparingly.

  indigo skies behind us

  with fluffy pale clouds

  intermittently spread around.

the droplets of noise

trickling down the porch mesh

and onto the wooden sills.

bright overhang fan,

a light breeze through your hair

amidst the walled room.

sitting in wicker furniture,

you in my arms,

happy.

dodie in the background-

she always made me think of you.

well, makes, not made,

cause even now,

you still appear in my thoughts.

even now,

i can't forget.

i won't forget.

 please don't forget.

i can't go on.

without the promise.

 of us together again.

grief is weird.

every day, my brain takes me back to

   when i needed her most.

when there was a   family unit,

   fifteen adolescents in a room—

   we bickered and fought (like teenagers do)—

     it was all so

       useless.

years later, the family unit

        crowds around me—

  "text me if you need to",

    "feel free to reach out",

 i guess they didn't mean it.

unopened texts and unanswered calls—

i follow-up, with "i'm okay"

but i guess they wouldn't care regardless.

is this how you'd have reacted

if it were me in that casket?

maybe she was right about you.

maybe she was right about a lot

of things.

she deserved better.

she deserves better.

it's not too late to do better.

for some, i guess it is.

<u>lion head fountain</u>

meet me at the lion head fountain.

your class lets out

the same time as mine.

we'll sit in your room,

put on a record,

and mourn the day

together.

two boys lay

in a corner-sized closet,

one on another,

a foundation for the shorter.

my head lays

on your shoulder.

i rest in your aura.

i could die in your embrace.

hell awaits me

outside these cornered walls;

this but a reprieve.

you are my early grave.

the record plays.

i barely hear it.

<u>immersion</u>

i sit, in a theatre

with dim lighting and pews

the cast sits ahead of me, calm before the storm.

they chit chat and wait

for the show to begin.

i reminisce as i remember

this longing feeling.

again, we flashback,

but here, we go deeper—

before auburn plooms and autumn skies.

the broken boy finds solace around

three walls and an opening.

he crafts props to create a world

that is plastic and petite,

yet feels more real

than the   bleakness he feels.

i feel at home

amongst these theatre kids.

cardboard props and styrofoam settings—

these are   the makings of a memory.

how could i forget it?

no matter.

i'm home.

<u>translucent skin</u>

never meet your idols, they say—

they can't hold up to

your godly perspective.

alas, fate is cruel—

i run into them regardless.

my soul adjusts to your flaws.

aging eyes, thinning hairs,

hide the true faults lying beneath them.

you cower behind your wire frames

and i stare through your back, poised to attack.

you wouldn't look me in the eyes—

i stare harder.

i'll never forgive you

for what you   became—

i'll never forgive you

for the roles you played.

looking back, it's clear;

you're not the gods i once made you out to be.

your passivity killed her.

but, well, so did mine.

<u>sheeran</u>

dark blue and tan,

the colors of our love,

cover our bodies as we dress

for a dance.

we stumble towards the venue,

your grip on me tight—

we will make it through this

adventure.

confetti falls as we slow dance to sheeran.

you drunkenly gaze into my eyes,

the substance of love—

i love the way you

pronounce my name

as the glitter in your eyes trickles down

your cheek—

the party erupts around us,

i don't notice.

later in the night,

after admissions and remissions,

we persist in our desires and

proclaim love for the ages.

i will marry you, someday.

we kiss with our colors.

<u>empty corner</u>

the broken boy is back;

again, you watch as he emerges

   windswept hair and, button-down shirt

seeking to make right

   the wrongs he can't undo.

   broken boys   become   muttering men

you cringe as he meanders into maturity

   searching for a way

to appease his grievances

   how did he get here?

   you watch as he chants

lessons   to the wretched;

lines, you eye him

   sputter, about

   forgiveness   and forgetting.

   you wonder, will he ever

play it back

    and believe them?

his friends, they make up the corners;

his foundations founded by

    the friends frowned upon.

you wonder how he feels

    when the foundation split

beneath him.

    no matter.

he continues—

<u>am i?</u>

everybody   hates   me

today.

i get   glares

from

the   girls

in   the   gallows,

the

maskless

boys   on   the bus,

the

man   on   the sidewalk.

my laptop   is   dying.

i   go to   charge   it.

a girl   sits

where   i want to.   she   glares—

no.

stares.

she knows me,

she says.

we went to high school together.

i don't know her.

she seems nice.

why do i think

the world

hates me?

am i

the one

to blame?

<u>god, let me bleed</u>

many men

  melt in my mind.

to pick one is trifling.

    i feel   almost   nothing.

  love is formulaic.

    to fall in   love   after   years

  of time.   to take years.

      was it love if it was

        born out of necessity?

is that the only procedure   for love?

    i have no time

      for this.

  time, i'm running out.

    my youth is fading

  faster than a bullet. it will kill me if

i can't find

     a shield.

to ponder for years

     about   love and loss.

    when you've exhausted a topic

    so much, at what

point have you reached

       the end of it?

how could love exist

   if it's only   a concept

       in my mind?

have i dissected love so much

  that i no longer   see it

   without stitches?

    . . .

i'm too big for these britches,

          these bitches

      that torment my mind.

satan, dispose of me

       before the wickedness   sets in.

      i see it now—

god made us in his image,

     but not be a gift,

      or a narc's mirage,

        but as a plea

     to be freed from an

empty sea of

        shattered thoughts.

intelligence slices my skin—

       i bleed with god.

            (we drown together)

<u>technicolor astronaut man</u>

i lost

my bright pink

astronaut man

keychain.

the spot

it   usually   sits

was left

dormant.

do you   remember

when we got   him?

when   we   screeched

karaoke   at

our   formal—

harmonious,   despite

everything.

the gospel chords.

i hear them,

even   now.

the harpsichord of

the incoming marimbas;

vibraphones   pounding away   at their

sadistic   tendencies.

let them   shatter the glass

of your practice room   windows—

soundwaves   so   strident

they   BURST

through   your   eardrums,

like sticks through a snare.

the blood trickles from our   ears

like   the truck metal   in your abdomen,

flam tap   flam tap

bass   drum

ROLL.

get out getout get out getout GET

— sorry.

where   was   i?

o h .

.   .   .

it was only a keychain.

<u>i still get her letters</u>

life goes on after a death of a friend

   it feels like it shouldn't

  her interests, i keep finding

like letters she sent

   mailed from when she left us.

how dare they, how dare we

    change when she isn't here to see it.

  how much i wanted to show you my art.

i didn't realize then, i realize now——

   they were addressed to you.

 i must have forgotten

      to stamp them.

  i think they have letters in heaven.

and if they do,

    i hope she's sending them.

<u>florida boy</u>

i've never known this feeling

(i've always known this feeling)

i guess i've forgotten

how it feels

to fall in love

(it's been a while.)

i could live a life with you;

in another life, i already have

our souls have danced this dance

for eons—

do i choose to continue

or risk the lonely road?

i want to love you, live you,

learn you, lavish in your light like a cat

basking in a bay window.

how my heart flutters

when you grab my hand.

the passion that is fueled by your

intimate grasp.

two romantics in a room,

drowning.

i sink in your arms, my armoire,

a treasure chest paradise designated for me

and me alone.

i didn't mean to fall in love—

it wasn't on purpose.

just one day, i stopped writing about her

and started writing about you.

<u>dayton, ohio</u>

i stand,

dressed in grunge,

the people i once pleased

around   me.

where am i?

hear the marimbas,

longing for my youth,

yet   lacking a memory

to connect to.

"i feel nothing."

where are the emotions

i'm so used to evoking?

the romantic in me is

quiet today.

does he have nothing

to add?

here   i am,

wearing   the clothes

of a dead man,

retracing the steps of

the person   i once was—

hear the jeers, the drums,

the makings

of a memory

i never made.

is this what she was missing?

is this what sent her down

the chordic line?

cymbals crashing, hills descending to hell–

major to minor scales

finding power in an

all too quaint gym.

is this what

she died for?

it's all so— *underwhelming,*

though i suppose

that's to be   expected

when   depression

levels your thoughts.

i feel nothing for this place.

wishing she was here,

grieving what could have been—

what might have been.

knowing i don't belong.

perhaps it's for the best.

don't pin your hopes

on forgotten dreams.

<u>gold</u>

a midnight monologue

   feeds my mind

  as i beg to drift into space.

   sleep would ease these thoughts, and yet

  i can't help but let them wander.

  i saw her.

it's a weird thing to reminisce,

  her auburn ploom now blackened

and soaked in rich witch green.

   she's shorter than i remember—

perhaps i grew

  while we were apart

(though i don't feel much taller)

i loved her.

not well, it seemed.

platonics are hard to decipher

when the people push you together.

if only if i had known what i knew now—

that love is not always romantic.

if only i knew

that the strongest loves never fade,

no matter how hard you try.

i miss her.

oh, to be where you are right now,

amidst marchers and mellow mellos—

memories being made, mine but a memory.

thoughts evoke in my mind,

etching themselves in the upper echelons

of this echoey chamber.

they wreak havoc, and

remind me of her

departing message—

"nothing gold can stay"

(they read)

now i know it to be true.

i just wish she knew too.

<u>angelina</u>

it's been a month.

the crimson coffin we left you in

stays ever present in my mind.

you haunt me

like an angel to the guarded,

like a lion to its prey.

worst of all,

the silence continues.

i will always remember your hands

folded on your chest.

i will always remember

the angelic angle in which you laid.

i will always remember your pink-faded hair

tied back,   in a bun, so gorgeously strung.

i will always remember you.

the broken boy mourns you.

he mourns alone.

he was right; no one knew you

like he did.

how jarring that that was once

a point of pride.

the avalanche   has slowed,

but i pray to god

it never stops.

he doesn't want to be in pain—

he doesn't want to forget you.

how to balance both,

he ponders,

without splitting   his soul in two.

"i never loved you more

than when you said goodbye."

angelina.

may you rest among the stars.

<u>apology</u>

kathy.

i understand if you   don't respond,

                    i probably wouldn't.

this is a letter i should've written a long time ago.

when she died, i realized   just

 how much   i left   unsaid with her.

i don't know where to send her letter.

                              . . .

    & i hate that.

              & i can't bear the same   happening with you.

i want closure

    even if that means   never

          being able

            to see

             you

             again.

i just don't want to regret the things

i left unsaid any longer

    i'll never have the words to express what i feel.

  regret   is probably the closest,   I

    regret   the months we didn't speak.

       i loved you.

     maybe i still do.

i still hate you for what you did.

    i'm still sitting on that porch, waiting.

        i still see you in my dreams.

            i still miss you   like hell.

    . . .

                but i love him more.

for what it's worth,

i'm sorry for any pain i caused you.

i hope your auburn ploom returns.

signed,

the morning mourner

<u>two am walc</u>

"it's cold."

. . .

"i told you- you need a warmer coat."

"it's fine."   "i'm fine."

. . .

"the sky's pretty."

"yeah."

"you can really see the stars tonight."

. . .

"it's march. it shouldn't be this cold."

"here- take my coat. i'll take yours."

. . .

. . .

"i love you."

"i know."

. . .

"look at the stars."

. . .

"i wonder if she's among them."

<u>among the stars</u>

a bright constellation

rests in the sky—

my past awaits me.

the scene stirs

the memories in my amygdala

like dad's chili in the crockpot.

to see a niece, my sister's,

running up to me.

i lift her up and spin her

around the room—

festivals and speedways,

my groups gather.

families and marching bands,

mellow mellos and seniors and

that rich smell of independence

reprising itself.

i picnic with her again,

her letterman jacket draped over my back

as i shiver from the springtime air.

the stars settle above me,

and i feel at peace

knowing that there's

a reason i'm still here.

these sentences of senselessness,

these   dreams

aren't yet real

but still i feel

them achievable.

to envision a happy ending.

the loves of my life gather.

a wedding, a reception—

poems so

gorgeously strung

between floral centerpieces.

this is the life i've been waiting for.

i arrive.

acknowledgments

i don't quite know how to wrap up this debut novel- ironic as it is, i can never find the words to solidify how much a journey has meant to me. thus, I can only try my best (hopefully without getting too sappy).

for starters, i would like to thank my amazing parents, siblings, extended family and friends for their continued support of my writing journey. there are too many people i want to thank, so i'll just leave it at this— people are what fuel my experience. my dear friends, my family, my loves and my losses have all contributed to the creation of myself and my debut poetry collection. for that, i am so, so thankful.

secondly, i would like to thank everyone who helped contribute to this book. whether it be answering my endless questions about publishing, taking promotion photos or just listening to me drone on and on about word counts and page margins— i appreciate your support tremendously. i would like to credit the wonderful photographer holyn booher for the photos used on the back of and at the end of the book. you can find her at @holyndaze on instagram. furthermore, i'd like to give a special shoutout to my beta readers; in no particular order, thank you to grace gochnauer, margaret slover, noah mueller, leif blake, marissa oatess, anna wrobel and taylor mccartney. love you guys!

i want to give a huge shoutout to gavin zyonse (a.k.a. the other half of this book) for being my muse and for helping me with all the behind-the-scenes work that goes into formatting, editing and publishing a book. i truly could not have done it without you. thank you so much for always being in my corner and for being my other half. i love you, florida boy.

i would like to give one final acknowledgement to my dear friend autumn martin, whom this book is dedicated to. i could not have done this without you. you lifted me up in so many ways; i only hope to return the favor and honor and encapsulate your charm and lovely spirit. you were such a gift to this world, and you will continue to be a gift to it via the people on this earth that love and miss you. this one's for you, aut.

with that, that leaves you, my dear reader. thank you for following along with me on my poetic journey. if you liked the collection, feel free to leave a review. i hope you had a fun time reading! from one morning mourner to another— i'm learning that the best things in life come from taking chances. thank you for taking a chance on a young romantic with an affinity for writing and a dream.

as always, here's to more letters.

signed,

the morning mourner

about the author

zachary hodges currently lives in west lafayette, indiana, where he is a rising sophomore at purdue university and working towards a degree in english education. when he's not at college, he lives with his parents dr. kim hodges and mr. steve hodges in greenwood, Indiana. he has four siblings- bailey, madison, andew and dalton- who he loves very much. outside of writing, zack is passionate about musical theatre, travel, activism and second-hand fashion. while this is his first book, he sincerely hopes that this will not be his last. you can follow his journey at @themorningmourner on instagram, as well as his website at https://zacharyhodgesbooks.wixsite.com/my-site.